# Living Beyond Obedience

A different approach to living with dogs

Tracy Franken 2019                    2nd Edition

# Preface ........................................................................ 4
## *A dog named Jayce* .................................................... *4*
# Introduction to LBO ................................................. 8
### Getting Started ........................................................................ 9
# BE With ...................................................................... 10
## *To BE or Not to BE* .................................................... *10*
### What is BE With? ................................................................. 10
### Things to observe: ................................................................ 11
### Some Notes on BE With: ....................................................... 12
# Foundation of Relationship™ Framework (F.O.R.) .................................................................... 15
## *The beginning of a beautiful relationship...* ............ *15*
# Leadership ................................................................. 16
## *It always comes back to leadership* ........................ *16*
### The Leadership Score Card ................................................. 18
### Where we humans lose our points ..................................... 20
### When does the Leadership Score Card come into play? ................ 21
# Relevance and the Relevance Score Card ......... 23
## *How "relevant" are you to your dog?* ..................... *23*
### The Relevance Score Card .................................................. 23
# Fulfilment Factor ..................................................... 29
## *It's more than just exercise* ...................................... *29*
# Play Drive .................................................................. 34
## *The way to your dog's Fulfilment Factor.* .............. *34*
## *What equipment do you need to tap into the drive?* ........ *37*
# Situational Learning ............................................... 42

*4 areas of your dog's life* ...................................................*42*

# Recall ...............................................................46
*It's a long term relationship goal* ...........................*46*

# Food Drive, Motivation and The NILFF Program 50
*What does this mean for your relationship?* .....................*50*
### How To Build up Food Drive: .....................................54

# The Fearful Dog ...............................................56
*" People are strange when you're a stranger..."* ................*56*
### The "OMG; I am going to die!" Moment: .......................59
### The "Ahhh I Didn't die" Moment: ..............................62
### "Take the time it takes so eventually it takes less time" .............64
### Living with a Fearful Dog ......................................65
### Layered Stress ..................................................68

# The Confident Dog ..........................................71
*And it's not about dominance* .................................*71*

# The Right Brain/Left Brain Introvert/Extrovert discussion ........................................................74
*A different way to look at your dog* .............................*74*
### THE LEFT BRAIN ..............................................75
### THE RIGHT BRAIN ............................................75
### INTROVERT .....................................................75
### EXTROVERT .....................................................75
### The Horses That Showed me the Way .........................78

# Conclusion .......................................................81
*The journey to a better relationship has just begun.* ..........*81*

# Preface
## *A dog named Jayce*

This is the story of a dog named Jayce and how he changed my life. I will continue to carry the lessons that Jayce taught me for years to come.

**The day I met Jayce**
 On February 24 2018, I boarded a plane headed to Dallas Fort-Worth, Texas.  The purpose of the trip classified as a business trip but would later be changed to "Life-Altering" if there was such a classification.  This trip was a highly anticipated one.  The criteria:  to "experience living with a dog." A dog that was new to me for nine days.  The rules:  No crates, no training tools, and 100% living with the dog.  (Later translated to: you have to take the dog in the shower with you because you can't trust him to stay on his own for 10 minutes)  The dog: A young adolescent husky named Jayce. The description from the rescue which currently had him.  " He was too mouthy for his current owners."

## THE DAY WE GOT THE HUSKIES

We arrived at the daycare boarding facility where the huskies were staying. The dogs were let out into a small outdoor area one at a time while the rescue and volunteers gave us their information about each dog. Some were shy/quiet, some polite, some were distant and dismissive. Jayce, well he came out like a freight train, jumped up on almost every person there. He did not, however, jump on me but, that was merely luck on my part as he found something on the ground to sniff allowing me to scratch his butt and therefore keeping his feet on the ground. However, just as I thought I avoided the inappropriate advances of this very bold and cocky dog, he immediately proceeded to thrust his head up the front of my coat and grab at my shirt underneath. (What?!?!)

Jokes made all around by the other people in the course, but I knew there was no way I wanted this dog as my "husky buddy" for the week. So what happened? Well, because I was sharing a rental car with my friend Karen, the rescue wanted to make sure we would have compatible dogs that can share a car ride, and as luck would have it... I got Jayce.

We had a short session of introduction and walking with the dogs before we had to load them up into the cars and head to the centre to pick up all the supplies and food we needed for the week.

Karen tied her dog Osha in the back of our Jeep Patriot, and I decided I would sit in the back seat and hold on to Jayce for the trip.

Jayce proceeded to try and crawl on my lap, bite at my arms, face and whatever else he could get a hold of to try to get to Osha in the back. I am getting a little more than frustrated, and we couldn't get to the training centre fast enough. Luckily there we were able to let the dogs have a nice peaceful walk in the country. We could both de-stress and re-set. Which apparently would be short-lived. When we got to the hotel, that is when I broke down and cried. Well, that is a story for another day...

This book is dedicated to all the dogs that allowed me to live in their world, even if for just a moment.

To my family, for putting up with a life with dogs. (many, many, dogs)

To my husband Mark, the man that never says no to me. (why else would we have so many dogs?)

And to my mentor and friend Nelson Hodges. Thank you for 'seeing' me.

*Don't teach the dog, reach the dog*
            *~Nelson Hodges*

# Introduction to LBO

Thank you for your interest in creating a deeper, more meaningful relationship with your dog.  I hope you find the journey as joyful and rewarding as I do.  I want to point out that the work I do in and at Beyond Obedience is in no way meant to replace modern day obedience training.  What you learn through the Beyond Obedience program is intended to enhance your current practice, OR if you have not yet started a training program with your dog, Beyond Obedience will be the foundation upon which you can build your training.  (Training will be a breeze once you start implementing the information you learned here).  It is essential to understand that "obedience" is English as a second language to your dog.  In other words,  the dog must understand what the human wants (when I say this English word, I need you to do this action). Beyond Obedience is the expectation of the human to understand what the dog NEEDS.   It is a different angle to approach living with your dog.  And if we (humans) are  the more intelligent species (I know that is debatable), then doesn't it make sense for us to try to understand our dogs?  Stephen Covey in his book "The 7 Habits of Highly Effective People" said "Seek first to understand, then to be understood" I believe this to be true with any communication but even more so when trying to communicate with another species.

Ideas discussed in this book are what works for my pack and me, in my situation right now. The thoughts are meant as suggestions or points to ponder. What you decide to implement in your own life, is yours to determine. Let every action you take be the product of your own conclusion. Just as we will discuss leadership, later on, don't be a follower in your own life (or your dog's) but rather implement the information that works for you and your dog. Enjoy!

Getting Started

Now whether you have worked with me privately, attended one of the workshops or have taken my online courses Relationship Remedy™, or Living Beyond Obedience: The Essentials, these notes will complement what we have discussed. If you are new to me, a very warm welcome as we begin this journey together.

As always you can find me on Facebook [www.facebook.com/BeyondObedience](www.facebook.com/BeyondObedience)

or visit my website: www.beyondobedience.ca

# BE With
*To BE or Not to BE...*

The first thing I like to talk about when we are going to delve into your relationship with your dog is an exercise called BE WITH. We need to know where you are before we can figure out where you are going. Now, where you are might be ok, but we still need to know.

This was an exercise I originally learned from Pat Parelli's Natural Horsemanship when working with my horses and believe me when I say it changed my relationship with my horses for the better. Later with the help of the information, I learned from my mentor Nelson Hodges, I adopted this to be an exercise you can do with your dog.

I want to start by stressing that there is no right answer or outcome for this exercise (even though there seems to be). Trust me— this is 100% a "How Interesting " exercise. And even if you get some feedback you weren't' expecting or may seem disappointing, remember, this is the beginning of your journey. Things WILL get better.

## What is BE With?
Simply put, I want you to BE with your dog. But WAIT! There are rules!

1. There is no talking to the dog
2. There is no touching the dog
3. Try to sit at the dogs level in a familiar (but not too familiar) enclosed area. ( i.e., don't do this in your living room because your dog may just find his bed and go to sleep)
4. Observe what your dog does in your presence when you are not talking, touching, or otherwise micromanaging his behaviour. (How interesting!!!)

## Things to observe:

- Does your dog "check-in"?
- Does your dog settle down? How fast?
- Where do they sit? ( How close to you?)
- Where does your dog go?
- How do they sit (facing you, facing away from you?)
- Does your dog lie down? (how close to you, body position, etc)

- How do they lay down? (On their hip? On their haunches? Facing you? Facing away from you?)
- Did your dog try to get you to pay attention to them ( pawing, barking, whining, etc.)
- Did your dog try to sit or lie on top of you?
- Did your dog calm down quickly, or were they restless?

## Some Notes on BE With:

Again, there is no right or wrong here. (And now here is where I make you feel there is a right or wrong but bear with me). We are looking to see if your dog has some "pro-social" behaviour. Dogs that are interested in the pack rather than only looking after or fulfilling themselves are pro-social. Examples of pro-social behaviour would be:

- Your dog calms down and hangs out with your when you sit down
- Your dog settles somewhat close to you ( in the same room, near you)
- Your dog positions himself facing in the same direction (we're together) OR
- Your dog positions himself next to you but facing the opposite direction ( I have got your back).

- When the dog lies next to you, he is relaxed and not on alert (I feel safe around you).

**What if your dog doesn't do these things?**

A dog that chooses to sit away from you or do their own thing may be a dog that is a little more independent. If the dog sits a distance away from you (out of arms reach) and is facing you, it could mean "I don't trust you." I will see this positioning when I am working with a client dog. It makes sense because we haven't built up a relationship yet. In contrast, a dog that is sitting away from you and not facing you may mean " I don't care about you, you pose no threat to me" Still not sure what your dog is saying? Feel free to reach out to me on social media or consider joining my premium program Relationship Remedy. (We discuss BE With results at length inside the course)

See how interesting? Now, what if you have a dog that isn't displaying pro-social behaviour? Well, read on my friend and find out how you can turn this whole thing around.

Connor and Rue
"BEing" with.
BE with doesn't have to be an exercise you set out to do, but rather taking a moment out of your busy day. Quieting the mind and BE with each other.

# Foundation of Relationship™ Framework (F.O.R.)
*The beginning of a beautiful relationship...*

The Foundation of Relationship Framework is where we begin our journey into a more empathetic connection and bond with our dogs. By working through and understanding the concepts within the F.O.R. framework, you will start to "see your dog in a whole new way."

The F.O.R. Framework consists of 3 foundations.

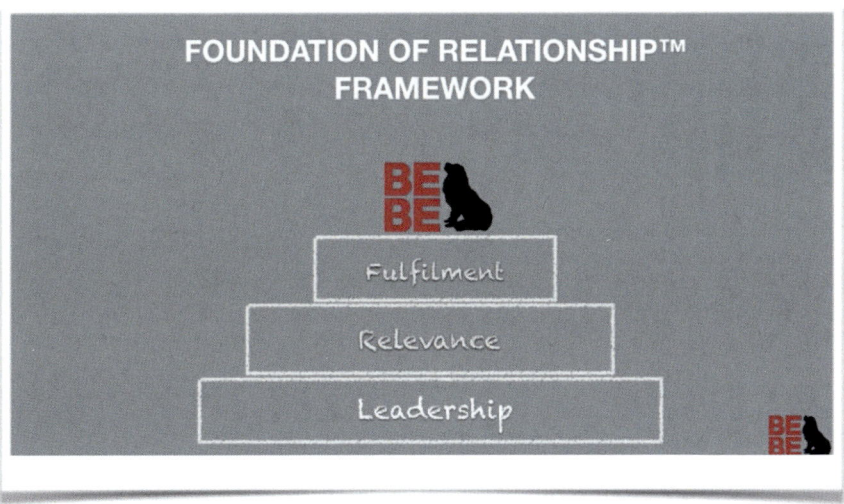

*The very first foundation block is* **LEADERSHIP.**

# Leadership
*It always comes back to leadership*

I think it is important to define "leadership". Webster Dictionary defines it as:

**LEADERSHIP**: *"the action of leading a group of people or an organization"*

*" the state or position of being a leader"*

**LEADER**: *"the person who leads or commands a group"*

When talking about dogs, I always think of leadership in the form of guidance. As in: I have to guide this creature through Humansville. In Humansville, we have very seemingly arbitrary rules that make no sense to the canines. Rules like:

- pee outside but don't pee inside
- chew this toy that looks like a shoe but not the actual shoe; and,
- chew this wood stick but not this wooden table leg.

You get my point.

I mean when you think about it, how do dogs get along so well with us anyway? When you consider they are a completely different species (canines) living amongst people (primates), it seems only reasonable that we should include guidance (leadership) to our canine friends. Right?

*What does it mean to be a leader to your dog?*

You have to **BE** someone worth following. Take a moment to let that sink in for a minute. Are you someone worth following? What makes you someone worth following?

**TRUST**.

It sounds simple, doesn't it? But it isn't always that way. For your dog to trust you, you have to be both **calm** and **predictable.**

You have to be able to handle all stressful situations without getting stressed out. (Not so simple now is it?).

Today in our busy, stressed-out lives, we unknowingly lose trust with our dogs. Had a bad day at the office? Are the kids driving you crazy? Money drama causing you stress? Hey, I get it. Heck, I'm living it. By understanding how our stressful lives and emotions can affect our trustworthiness, we can see the deficits we are creating in our relationships with our dogs. Awareness is the first step to real change.

## The Leadership Score Card

It is always fun to make it into a game and to add a scorecard. I mean, how else will you know how well you are doing, right? So here are the rules of the game;

**EVERY TIME YOU DO SOMETHING FOR YOUR DOG, I WANT YOU TO ASK YOURSELF:**

*Was that my idea and the dog followed through?*

OR

*Was that the dog's idea and I followed through?*

✅ If it was the **DOG'S** idea and you followed through, the **DOG** scored a point.

BUT

✅ If it was **YOUR** idea and the dog followed through, then **YOU** scored the point.

## Leadership Score Card Example

| DOG | ME |
|---|---|
| **asked to go out (1)** | Made him sit before he went out (1) |
| **asked to play ball (1)** | Started the game and ended the game on my terms (1) |

The points are for EVERYTHING you do for the dog. EVERY. THING.

Now you don't actually have to keep a scorecard (although some people have), but this will make you aware of what is going on in your house. If you are currently struggling with **any** aspect of your dog's behaviour, there is a good chance you are LOW on LSC points. (your dog is winning 😜)

## Where we humans lose our points

We lose points when we 'do' things for our dogs that wasn't our idea. Things like:

- Feeding on the dogs' terms
- Treating or rewarding on the dogs' terms or for no reason
- Being dragged down the street on the leash ( unless that was your idea)
- Letting them outside (even though you "taught" them to indicate when they have to go out, technically if they get you to move your feet...point to the dog)
- Chasing them in a game of retrieve or fetch *** he who moves who's feet, scores the point in play
- Affection ( this is a BIG one. Giving affection on the dogs' terms is where most of us kind-hearted humans lose points... I mean how can you resist?)

BUT ALSO

- Giving space (letting your dog have your space on furniture, or even walking around your dog when they are in your path)
- Micro-movements (i.e. dog jumps at you and your lean back to avoid getting punched in the face... your dog scored a point)

*How many ways are you losing points?*

## When does the Leadership Score Card come into play?

*ONLY WHEN IT MATTERS.*

When your dog has a decision to make (i.e. recall when there is a squirrel in sight), the card will come out. And if you are low in points, there is an excellent chance your dog is NOT going to come back when you call. Why would he?

The scorecard comes out anytime you want to or need to influence your dog's behaviour.

The scorecard comes out in the moments your dog has a fearful response, and you are trying to calm him down. If you are low in points, your dog is NOT going to be soothed by your words or actions at that moment. Why would he?

The scorecard comes out when your dog is barking and alerting, and you ask him to be quiet because there is no need to bark, but if you are low in points he will not believe that you have this situation under control. Why would he?

The scorecard will come out whenever your dog is questioning his safety and survival.

## *How is your LSC?*

*The second foundation block is* **RELEVANCE**

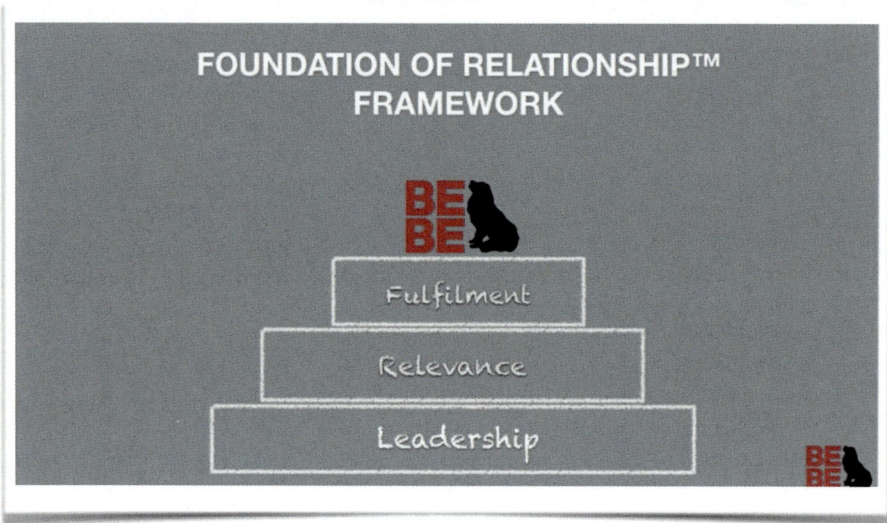

# Relevance and the Relevance Score Card
*How "relevant " are you to your dog?*

I love my scorecards and my definitions:  Webster defines:

RELEVANCE: "the quality or state of being closely connected or appropriate"

I like everything about this definition.  Closely connected, appropriate... nice!

## The Relevance Score Card

The **Relevance Score Card** is a little more challenging to score. Consider two extremes on opposite sides of the scale. One side we call the "dog-like" side. And on the other side is the "human side" The middle of the scale being an equal balance of both. (Sweet Spot).  When figuring out your relevance score with your dog, you first have to determine where you and your dog are on the scale.  It is important to note many factors determine this. For you, your physical abilities or limitations can contribute to your placement on the scale. It's important to be honest when determining where you are on this scale.   For your dog, the breed will play a huge role in where they are on the scale. So, once you figured out where you and your dog are on the scale, the "gap" between you is your relevance score. Now again, just like the LSC, you don't actually have a number or a score to keep. This is an exercise in awareness. If you are on the far end of the human-like side of the scale and your dog is on the dog-like side of the scale, you and your dog are going to struggle with relevance. Now, there are ways to bridge that gap. (YES!) If you want the dog to slide across the scale toward the more "human-like" side, you are going to have to teach your dog more **OBEDIENCE.** This will help your dog cope and suspend his dog-like instincts over there in Humansville. However, you don't want your dog to do ALL the work, right? So for you the human, to slide your way down the relevance scale, you need to have more **UNDERSTANDING**. More understanding of the dogs' innate drives and desires. You need to come out of your house, get into nature and experience the world (a little) the way your dog does.

So how does one start to move the needle down the scale to be more "dog-like"?

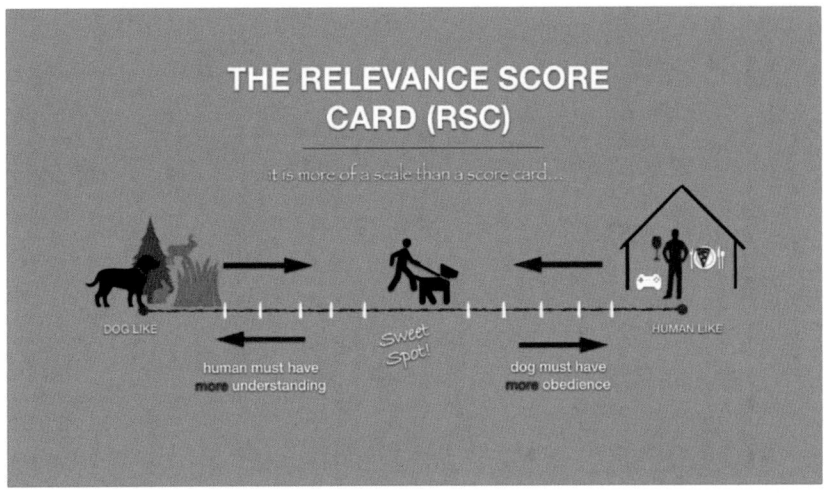

Essentially asking, "how relevant am I to my dog?" Beyond just loving him or giving treats, how else can you gain relevance points in the dog's mind? What is vital to your dog?

*hint: it's not giving your dog lots of love*

Dogs are all about survival. And if you don't believe me, consider how well dogs have adapted to humanity to get as far as they have. Dogs nowadays have the best orthopedic beds, Egyptian cotton blankets and organically produce dog food. So adaptation and survival are in their DNA. Now, you may think that you automatically gain relevance points when you provide for all the survival things your dog needs like food, water, shelter, and pack social stuff (incidentally also affecting your leadership scorecard). But remember what you think makes you relevant may not be what your dog thinks makes you relevant.

Here is my favourite quote from Bruce Fogle's A Dog's Mind

> *"A dog doesn't expect to be treated like a human. A dog expects a human to act like a dog, to participate in group activities, to play, to hunt together, to sleep in the same den."*

When you think about that, ask yourself; Are you meeting up to your dog's expectations?

- Have you gone on a hunt lately with your canine companion?

- When you play, are you playing like a dog? Practicing the kill? ( See Play Drive Chapter )

- Are you going on a ritual of migration and exploration with your dog, or are you just taking him for a walk?

Now admittedly, I am not asking you to go and kill something with your dog? Well no, not unless that is something you are into. But have you considered bringing your dog's meal out on a walk and hiding it in the grass and then "finding it" together? Essentially hunting for the food? What about an adventure walk where you are interested in some of the things your dog is sniffing? (even the gross stuff!)

How do you play with your dog? Does it include you? Engaging with your dog on terms your dog values will drastically increase your Relevance Score Card. Just some things to think about.

It is important to note that your RSC is influenced by many factors and it may change throughout your relationship with your dog. For example, if you live in the city in an apartment building, you are living a more "human-like" existence. Your dog will need more obedience ( English as a second language) for them to be calm and balanced. And that is because there will be a lot more human rules and boundaries that your dog must comply with for you both to be happy in that environment. There is nothing wrong with this situation; it just means that you will have to put in more obedience training time here.

In contrast to that, if you live out in the country and have the opportunity to allow your dog a little more "dog-like" experience, then it is crucial to take some time to study and understand the drives of the dog and how to be a part of it. You will struggle for relevance with your dog if you are competing with nature, rather than being naturally a part of it. The goal would be to find a balance between the two, where both dog and human meet somewhere in the centre of the scale in that "sweet spot."

> Consider this...
>
> When taking your dog for a walk, do you:
>
> A. Grab the leash and go, make sure he does his business and get home because you have to make supper
>
> B. Take your time, let him check his pee mail and do his business
>
> C. Go on a exploration adventure with the dog, checking out the things he is sniffing, being engaged and interested in the walk ( ie not thinking about your shopping list or your to do list

*Where are you and your dog on the Relevance Score Card?*

---

*The third foundation is* **FULFILMENT FACTOR**

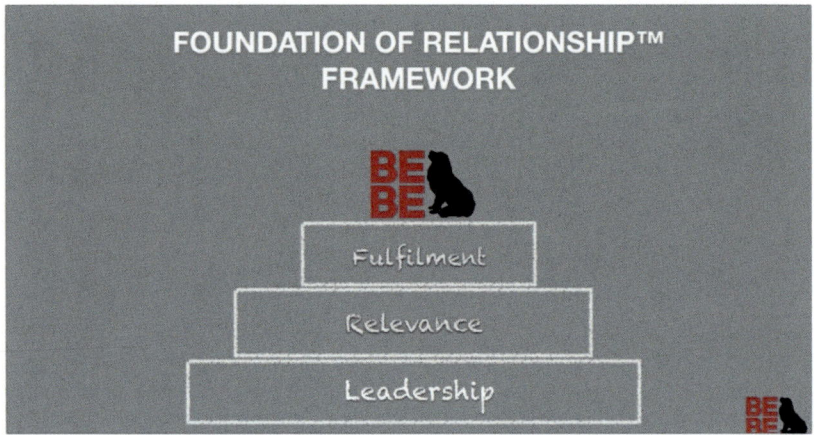

# Fulfilment Factor
*It's more than just exercise*

Webster's definition:

FULFILMENT: "the achievement of something desired, promised or predicted"

"satisfaction or happiness as a result of fully developing one's potential"

**Take a look at your dog right now. Is your dog "fully developing his/her potential"?**

The Fulfilment Factor is unique to every dog. It is also somewhat breed specific. It is not about exercising to tire out the dog but instead, it is about actual fulfilment.

Problems exist if the exercise that you are doing with your dog is NOT their F.F. you will only create an unfulfilled athlete. Quite often, people who struggle with destructive or frustrated dogs, the answer lies in Fulfilment Factor.

## THE STORY OF CHUCKLES

I have a lot of dogs. One day my husband came home with a Basset Hound puppy. My first response was not even no but, "oh HELL NO!" Now I should clarify by saying I have nothing against Basset Hounds. I do however know that I struggle with all hound type dogs simply because I am an A-type personality and I have a hard time walking the hound types when their walk seems to be governed by their nose. So because all of our dogs "work" here at Beyond Obedience I didn't see how a Basset Hound would be able to "help" us in our programs. However, my husband's puppy dog eyes were bigger and sadder than the puppy's so... Chuckles came to live with us. Now, at the time we  had 3 Newfoundland puppies about the same age so I put Chuckles in their group in the hopes that he would somehow learn to be a Newf. (Spoiler alert: he didn't). When we would go for our pack walks, I would sandwich him in between 2 Newfs so that he would be forced to focus on the walk rather than his nose. And for the most part, it worked! He walked like a charm between those dogs. During our walks, we have an "at liberty " time. This is the time when the dogs are free to sniff around and explore a little bit. With the Newfs, I would tuck their leashes in their collars and let them go. This was a signal to them that although they could explore around, they still had to be mentally checked in with me. However, once Chuckles came into my life, I knew I would not be able to just tuck in his leash and let him go. So I would give him the length of the leash and then begrudgingly walk along, letting him sniff and prevent him from pulling me into the ditch. Then, one day I thought to myself, "I am not being very fair to him." So I started to "follow" him into the long grass and down into the swampy ditch. But I didn't just follow him; I actively participated in the walk. If he sniffed a rock, I would turn it over saying things like, "what did you find?"

Now admittedly, it kinda freaked him out at first. After all this crazy human was following his every move. And he dragged me through some pretty disgusting terrain. BUT... What happened after was almost magical. Once we were done, and we came out of the ditch and gathered up the rest of the pack, Chuckles walked happily beside me the whole way home. No Newf sandwich required. He was thoroughly fulfilled.

You see, I believe that when our dogs live in a constant environment where they have to "follow" our rules, we miss out on so much more bonding and relationship building. What happens when you follow a dogs' rules for a while? Well, besides getting a little muddy, you get a dog that will follow you no matter what, even if their genetics tell them otherwise. That is pretty powerful stuff.

The old saying " A tired dog is a good dog" should be changed to " A fulfilled dog is a happy dog" (or something cooler than that!)

Find out your dog's fulfilment factor and you will see other behaviour problems diminish!

> **TIP!**
> Want an easy way to help figure out your dogs fulfilment factor?
> Find the moments where your dog is experiencing pure joy. Capture that. That is where the FF will be.

> How can you be a part of your dog's fulfilment?

*What is your dog's Fulfilment Factor?*

# Play Drive
*The way to your dog's Fulfilment Factor.*

Play drive is a very powerful drive to tap into, and when used properly, it feeds the **LEADERSHIP SCORE CARD,** the **RELEVANCE SCORE CARD,** and the **FULFILMENT FACTOR.** It is like the triple crown of relationship with a dog! (And here you thought it was just a silly game of fetch.)

The reason is it so powerful is that play drive is running parallel to PREY DRIVE. And because your dog is a PREDATOR, prey drive is pretty important yes?

So let's first look at the **PREDATORY MOTOR PATTERN** in dogs.

The predatory motor pattern is innate in all our dogs. Now through our selective breeding processes, we have managed to enhance or eliminate certain aspects of the pattern. The entire pattern is:

ORIENT > EYE STALK > CHASE > GRAB BITE > KILL BITE > DISSECT > CONSUME

Different breeds will have some parts of the pattern enhanced ( Eye stalk is enhanced in the Border Collie or the Australian Shepherd) while other parts of the patterned are removed or lessened ( Orient is enhanced in a Pointer, but eyestalk is removed and replaced but the "pointing" action ) When our dogs play they are actually tapping into the predatory motor pattern. Consider the games your dog plays. ( See diagram 1a)

So since play is mimicking the prey drive, you are essentially tapping into that impressive drive!

Now here is where you put the whole F.O.R Framework into "play."

- HOW you do Fulfilment Factor will affect your LSC. ( i.e. make sure you are starting and stopping the drive), and
- Being an active part of fulfilment factor will significantly increase your RSC.

*Win-Win-Win!*

Diagram 1a

## PREDATORY MOTOR PATTERN AND PLAY

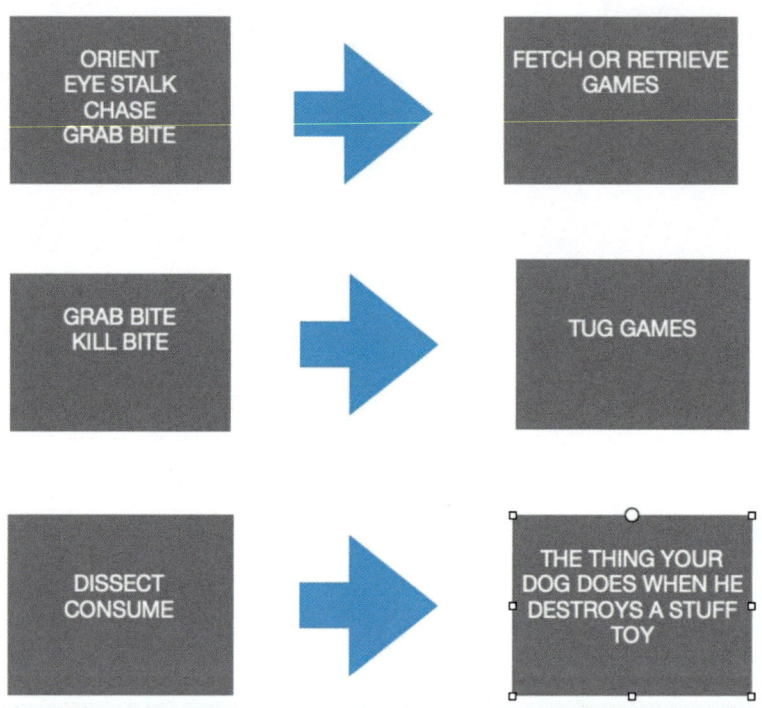

36

# Toys and Play Drive
*What equipment do you need to tap into the drive?*

I categorize my toys into 3 groups:

**1. Interactive Toys**

**2. Chew Toys**

**3. Squeaky Stuffed Toys**

**Interactive Toys**: (These include balls, frisbees, chuck it, tug toys, flirt poles, etc.) These toys should be just that —INTERACTIVE. Meaning they should include YOU. If your dog is running around throwing their tennis ball or tugging their tug toy on their own, you are missing the mark on these games and this drive. Here is a test. If you bring out the ball, what does your dog do? If he grabs it and runs around the yard with it, that joy your dog feels right then is about THE BALL and not you. Remember, your interactive toys are the medium used to embrace the drive. Without you, the toy should be meaningless (and boring). Usually, dogs that have learned to entertain themselves with a toy is because the owner checked out of the game. Don't let that be you!

Here are some tips to make sure you are part of the interactive toy games:

1. *Do not leave interactive toys out for your dog.* Put them away. This helps in a couple of levels. One, it ensures the game is always about you. Two, it makes sure the dog doesn't decide when he wants to play and therefore ensures you get the leadership scorecard points. ( Ahhh, don't forget the LSC!)

2. Make sure you start the game, you determine the rules of the game, and that they are followed, AND you stop the game. ( No pestering after to keep throwing the ball.)

3. For added leadership points, add some obedience stuff in the mix. Doing your obedience training during play makes training SO MUCH MORE FUN!

**TUG TIPS**:

The game of tug is a great way to build up points in **Fulfilment Factor**. Many "mouthy" dogs need an outlet for their mouths, and playing tug with your dog is a great way to do that. Also playing tug is very "dog-like" so your **Relevance Score Card** goes through the roof with this awesome game! Here are some tips for the tug lovers out there!

1. First, if you are going to teach the game of tug, expect to get bit. It's a given. Dogs have great control and aim, but more often than not the hu-

man is not great at presenting a good target.

2. Make sure your tug toy is sturdy and has room for the dog to grab, but not too long that you can't control the toy ( i.e., don't get a huge long rope when you are first teaching the dog to tug.)

3. Tug has 3 obedience terms the dog needs to learn ( what you choose to call each component is your own choice), i.e. "take it" "out" "yes."

4. Always be sure to "present the toy" in a way the dog will succeed.

5. Give the 'take it' command and pull the toy AWAY from the dog. (It has to act like prey, and prey doesn't generally jump into the dog's mouth).

6. Let the dog win every once in a while. Your dog will not want to keep playing with you if he never wins.

7. To teach the "out" command you essentially "kill" the toy. Dead prey is no more fun, so say "out," kill the toy, and then wait. As soon as your dog releases the toy, say "yes" and present it immediately again. You don't want to end the game every time you say "out" otherwise your dog will not want to ever OUT the toy. Your "out" command should mean, we get to start the game again!

8. You should end the game before the dog tires of the game. (Always leave them wanting more!)

**Chew Toys:** This seems self-explanatory but I am going to explain it anyway. Chew toys are just that; toys your dog chews on. HOWEVER, (this is where the explaining comes in 😜) I am talking about the toys/ bones that the dog really chews on. Like with their back teeth. You know that really good gnawing sort of chew? That chewing is a calming relaxing sort of chew. It is the equivalent (I believe) to the chewing that wild dogs would do on the leftover bones after a good kill. So these toys are great for calm, quiet times like crate time, or after a good play session and we are all just chilling out. This doesn't include the frantic front of the mouth chewing you see during a game of fetch where the dog doesn't want to give up the object and starts frantically chewing at it. That type of chewing is more of the scavenger panic that happens right after the kill when everyone is trying to get in on the feed!

**Squeaky Stuffed Toys:** If your dog DESTROYS squeaky stuffed toys, you should be aware that your dog is practicing THE ART OF KILLING AND DISSECTING. Yes, that is true. (And here you thought it was cute.) SO... My rule of thumb for my life with my dogs is: I don't allow my dogs to practice the art of killing something in my home. Full disclosure here; I started this back when my children were young, and the reason was that I never wanted my dogs to make that mistake of destroying the wrong toy and then having to explain to my kids why Barbie is headless, and that favourite teddy bear no longer has any eyes. But later in life, when I started understanding this predatory motor pattern and seeing how it relates to play... well, it just seemed to make sense to keep up with the "no killing things in my house" rule. However, that squeaky conflict is the heightened part of prey drive, and I would think if you wanted to up your leadership points and your relevance points (actually be involved in the hunting with your dog stuff) you could certainly do this, I just would want to make sure that I am engaged and in charge of it. So using a flirt pole and only doing this outside would be my suggestion. However, it is your life and your dog and your rules. To each his own.

# Situational Learning
*4 areas of your dog's life*

I will be the first to tell you that NONE of my dogs are obedience trained. That's right. None. (What?!?!?) And although I will admit that none of my dogs are obedience trained, I will also tell you that I have 19 really good dogs (#justgooddogs). Now part of the reason I can have 19 trained/untrained dogs has to do with where I live. I mean, I live in canine utopia. I don't have to deal with busy streets or noisy neighbours with yappy dogs, so I don't require my dogs to know a lot of obedience commands (English as a second language). However, the main reason why I can get away with having all these dogs, and no obedience is that I make my dog's life extremely simple. I can break down their life into 4 categories.

1.**WORK**: Leash walking for my dogs is their job. Really. Lots of times, their job is to pack walk with other dogs and be good role models. So when they are walking, they are working. No sniffing, no pulling, no goofing off. WORK. They know the moment their training collars and/or leashes are on they are working. (Incidentally, my dogs don't wear any collars at all at any other time so this procedure of leashing them up is a signal that they are going to work.)

**2.PLAY**: My dogs also know the moment they go into the play yard or the social arena, without any equipment on, that it is playtime. Be a dog. Run, play, get muddy. My body language changes to a more relaxed demeanour, and I have a playful attitude.

**3.EAT**: Now I would love to tell you that all my dogs patiently wait for their food and then all only go to their respective bowls when I call their names (wow that would take some obedience wouldn't it?) No, they don't. And I would be lying if I said it was calm. If you show up at my kennel at feeding time, you will know it! They get pretty excited. But that is okay. Feeding time is a celebration. Think of the wild dogs or wolves after a kill. It's a party. So I do allow my dogs to get excited about the fact that food is coming. However, they all know not to steal food from other dogs. Everyone is respectful. That is the bar I have set for them and it works for us.

4.**SLEEP/REST**: And then we have quiet time or rest time. Many people that came to my facility for an assessment were often quite amazed how peaceful the kennel was. And it was quiet because all of the dogs were resting. At night you will not hear a peep from our kennel (I wish I could say that about some of the other dogs in our neighbourhood.) The dogs know it is rest time and aside from the occasional "union meeting" ( a pack howling session that takes place a couple of times throughout the day), you will generally not hear them. Now I know what you are going to say ... "well that's fine for you Tracy, you have a kennel. How does this apply to my dog and me at home?" You see, I don't have all 19 of our dogs stay in my home (obviously because that would be crazy right?) However I do "rotate" the dogs in and quite often have 4-5 dogs in the house in the evenings. We usually keep the senior dogs inside, but we also rotate the younger dogs as well. We have one rule for our home, and that is: There is NO PLAYING IN THE HOUSE. Ever. Period. End of story. (even the puppies) I don't feel guilty about that. Why? Because they have had plenty of time to play outside in the play yard and my house is too small to have 3 kids and 4-5 dogs running around. But here is the thing. Because that is an expectation I have set for them AND I never break it, all the dogs know that as soon as they cross that threshold of the house, they are to be calm and lay down. Which means I don't have any chaos when people come over to visit. There are no accidentally chewing things they shouldn't because there are no toys in my house. There is no way for them to make bad choices because they are in a rest/calm state of mind. And it is accomplished by them understanding that is how they are to be in the house.

These are expectations that the dogs fully understand. Even visiting dogs will pick up on this very quickly because the rules never change. And this consistency helps the dogs to predict the outcome of their environment better, and by doing so, I have calmer, more peaceful dogs (and home.)

# Recall
*It's a long term relationship goal*

Recall is probably the number one thing most of my clients say needs work, (that and pulling on the leash). So I thought it would be a good idea to bring it up here as well. So let's look at recall from another angle.

*"Recall is a long term relationship goal, AND it is not easily transferable"*

What do I mean by that?

Long term relationship goal: Rome wasn't built in a day, and neither was your dog's recall. I am not talking about the obedience of recall but rather the behaviour of recall or the *"beyond obedience"* of recall (*oh snap, see what I did there?*). So after you have finished with the obedience of recall ( i.e., you have successfully taught the dog the meaning of the word COME), then it is time to work on the reliability of that recall. So let's go beyond the obedience (*oh man, there is just no stopping me now*) and break this down.

There are only 2 reasons your dog will come when they are called.

1. They want to      **OR**

2. They know they have to

Let's unpack this a little, shall we?.

They **WANT** to come to you:

Why would your dog want to come to you? Well, perhaps it is because you are holding onto or offering up something delicious, like your dog's favourite treat. Or maybe you have their favourite toy. Either one of these is an exchange-for-service sort of deal. They come, you give them something they want. It's a win-win.

Now the other less talked about method to get your dog to come when you call them, is just to be AWESOME... to your dog. You BE the REWARD.

**HOW TO BE AWESOME (TO A DOG):**

1) BE a great **leader** (i.e., always consider your Leadership Score Card)

2) BE **relevant** to your dog (by playing, hunting, eating, and sleeping in the same den)

3) BE **fulfilling** - honour your dog's genetic and innate qualities. Play to their strengths.

In other words... Follow the F.O.R. Framework.

Now, what about the second part?

They know that HAVE to.

Well, that means consequences. No one likes to talk about consequences; however, I think it is important to realize that consequences are not synonymous with punishment or pain. In fact, with my dogs, a consequence is as simple as a dirty look.

Now here is the cool part. Are you ready? You can work on BOTH sides of this motivation chart at the same time! It's true. You can do that by... You guessed it! LEADERSHIP!

That's right. Believe it or not, when you work on your Leadership Score Card daily, you are also working on RECALL. With proper leadership, dogs will naturally not only come when they are called but also tend NOT to go too far. They WANT to follow you because you are awesome and a great leader, but they also know that if they don't, there will be a fair consequence because that is what good leaders provide.

*Recall is not easily transferable.* This is also true. What this means is if you are working on your LSC all the time and your significant other is not.... well, your dog may not come back for your significant other. I have on occasion had people who are boarding their dogs with me tell me if I want to take their dog for an off-leash walk it is okay because their dog has an excellent recall. My response: "just because your dog comes back when you call doesn't mean he will come back when I call" And really when you think about it... why would he?

Be the reward.

# Food Drive, Motivation and The NILFF Program
*What does this mean for your relationship?*

Modern-day dog training includes the use of food and treats. Although I am not opposed or against this, it may, have some drawbacks when it comes to your relationship (in my opinion).

I was recently watching an excellent video on using food for motivation and training. It is a video by a very well- known and respected trainer. As I was watching the video, the instructor was talking about operant conditioning and classical conditioning, one thing that came up in his language time and time again was the word "manipulate." As in: "We use the food to manipulate the dog's behaviour." And for some reason, it stuck out for me as a negative, and I didn't like it. I don't want to 'manipulate' my dogs. So I looked it up in my Webster's dictionary …

MANIPULATE: to control or influence ( a person or situation) cleverly, unfairly or unscrupulously

Now I guess we can assume when working with dogs we are influencing "cleverly" rather than controlling unfairly or unscrupulously but still, it doesn't sound right. And yet, the language isn't wrong. I think that is precisely what we are doing when we are training our dogs; manipulating. Now don't get me wrong, I am not saying that we shouldn't train our dogs. We do need to have a shared language with our dogs, and obedience training is the way to do that. I just want you to consider HOW you are using your food and then utilize it to "cleverly influence" your dog's behaviour.

FOOD DRIVE: Food drive is about more than just how much your dog loves food, but that is a start. If you have a dog that picks at the food dish all day long, you know your dog has LOW FOOD DRIVE. But what is interesting is that even a dog that gulps down his food every time may still have a low food drive. Why is this? Well, when we are talking about food DRIVE, drives are based on survival. Wild dogs or wolves have high food drive because they know that if they don't catch that food now they don't know when the next time they will be eating. Their drive for the food is in their PREY DRIVE, and it will be substantial. But for your canine companions, well, they get a bowl of food for just waking up.

*"Hey there Fido, you just got up! Good boy, here's a bowl of food for your hard work."*

See, not quite the same drive as the hungry wild dog who just ran 1/4 mile to try and catch that rabbit. No, our dogs have grown quite accustomed to getting food twice a day no matter what and there is absolutely no effort required. So although your black lab practically inhales that bowl of food, his actual "drive" may still be down in the dumps.

I have attached this "Motivation Chart" to help demonstrate the importance of a good food drive, especially when it comes to motivation.

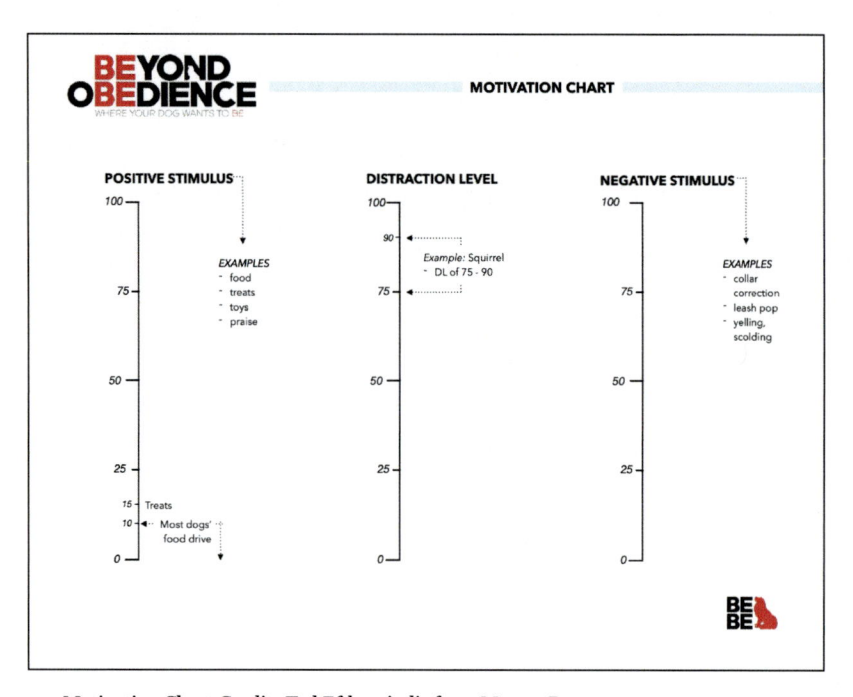

*Motivation Chart Credit: Ted Efthymiadis from Mango Dogs*

When we are talking about "motivation" we are talking about what it takes to motivate your dog's attention, engagement, check-in, whatever you want to call it, from a distraction ( in this example the distraction is a squirrel).  Now let's say, for your dog, a squirrel would be a distraction rate of 75- 90 on a scale of 0-100. If you notice where *most dog's food drive* sits on the positive stimulus side.  Sigh. Only a 10 or so.  You will also notice that treats are only at a 15 or so.  This explains why your food or treats will not work if your dog is distracted by a squirrel.  (Although they work great in low distraction areas like in your home).  Therefore at this moment, you will not be able to motivate your dog off the squirrel using food or treats.

Now it is important to note that there are only 2 ways you can motivate your dog off of a distraction.   You can:

1. Encourage the dog to come and get something they want (positive) or
2.  Apply or convey a consequence, which is something that they want to avoid (negative).

Most people who love their dog, want to work on the positive side of the motivation chart as much as possible (of course). This is the benefit of working on your dog's food drive if you want to use food or treats as a reward.

## How To Build up Food Drive:

Short answer: Make your dog work for their food. Getting your dog to work for that morning bowl of food drastically changes how they feel about the food. Now, you don't have to have your dog do obedience commands for every piece of food. I like to take that breakfast bowl on a morning walk. Hide some of it in the grass and go "hunt" for it together. Or do some recalls and engagement work out on your walk and reward with some of that breakfast. And you don't have to give it up one piece at a time. Do some variable rewards. High-value stuff gets a little jackpot of food, while simple, easy peasy stuff may only get one piece. This exercise also serves to up your LSC. Hand feeding, having your scent on the food, is you as a leader sharing your food. It also prevents or stops resource guarding of food when it comes only out of your hand. So many good things come from this one concept.

Now I understand that everyone is busy and perhaps you can't do a long training session every morning before work, that's why I am suggesting that you instead try to incorporate it into your morning walk. Even doing a little "feeding the chickens"* (throwing the kibble in the grass and having the dog find it) is a great way to get your dog to hunt for the food in the back yard and is a helpful step to building food drive.

**** always use caution when working with multiple dogs. Consult a trainer if you have dogs that will fight over food

I have known trainers that work with severely aggressive dogs (both human and dog aggression) that have used the NILFF program to help them completely rehabilitate a dog. Now most of you are not dealing with aggressive dogs so you don't necessarily have to use this program as a strict boot camp for your dog, but my hope is that you can start to understand that without high food drive your treat bag is going to be limited in how you can "manipulate" your dogs behaviour.

---

**TIP!**

Keep in mind, you won't gain any LSC or RSC points if you just throw the food in the back yard and then get ready for work. It has to be a "PRO-SOCIAL" event to get those points, so make sure you are part of the hunt!

---

# The Fearful Dog
*" People are strange when you're a stranger..."*

The Doors

If you have been in the dog training world like me, you have probably heard; most "aggression" is caused by fear and not dominance. In my experience, I would agree with this (for the most part). Most dogs that I have worked with that are acting aggressively, it has almost always come out of a place of being unconfident or fearfulness. I have only met a few dogs in my life that were aggressive and confident, and let me tell you those dogs will make the hair on the back of your neck stand up. Now admittedly, I choose not to work with a lot of aggressive dogs. My clients are mostly families and their family dog. Now that is not to say that these dogs don't "act" aggressively. They sure do! However, they are themselves not aggressive. There is a big difference. So what is with all the "fearful" dogs? I think my subheading from the song ♪ People Are Strange ♪♪ by The Doors sums it up nicely. We do have to remember that dogs are a different species, trying to cope in Humansville, and Humansville is a very strange and scary place for a dog. So what happens when you have a different species in a strange place run by an even stranger species? Well, without proper leadership and guidance, you are going to get some fearful, unpredictable behaviour.

Here is some food for thought.

Some dogs are just born innately fearful or unconfident. Just like people, dogs can be born innately confident or not. Let that sink in for a little bit. I mean really, you probably already know that is true, but yet, whenever we come across a fearful dog we want to know why. What happened in this poor dog's life that made them this way? Here's the thing. Perhaps nothing. And what if that were true, what does that mean for the naturally fearful or unconfident dog? Can we help them to become comfortable in Humansville?

The answer is YES.

Now there are lots of studies out there that will tell you other factors that contribute to the fearful dog, and I do not deny them necessarily, however, I think sometimes we look to the more complicated reasons instead of seeing what is right in front of us. I mean some people will go to great lengths to try and explain their dog's behaviour with stories like:

*"My dog was neutered too early and that is why she is fearful."*

or

*"Over vaccination is the cause of all the fear-aggressive dogs."*

or

*"My rescue dog must have had something horrible happen to him, and that is why he is so fearful."*

The problem with this type of discussion is that it leads us to believe that there is nothing we can do about it. That our dog is just going to *be* this way, and we will have to cater to our dog's emotional disability. And that is what fearful dogs can end up having- an emotional disability. What starts as perhaps an exaggerated natural response to a fearful stimulus, ends up being a life long trauma. But dogs aren't born traumatized . Us good-natured humans have cultivated it. It's sad when you think about it. And I am sure that is it also exhausting for the dog. Can you imagine living in fear your entire life? How tragic would that be?

So what can we do to help the naturally (and unnaturally) fearful dog? Well, I will start by saying I don't think you can "turn" a fearful dog into a confident dog. I believe that they will always be "innately fearful." However, what you CAN do is reduce the extremities of their reactions to a fearful stimulus. This means, your dog will still have the reaction of "OMG, I am going to die" however the "Ahhhh I didn't die" moment will come much quicker and easier when you start to understand them.

## The "OMG; I am going to die!" Moment:

I always like to use this analogy when talking about fear. Let's say you are coming home, and as you approach your house, you see your front door is ajar. At first, you are thinking, that's strange. I never forget to shut the door. As you enter your house, you hear a loud noise from upstairs. You know no-one is supposed to be home. Immediately your mind starts racing! Someone is in the house! Am I being robbed? What if that person is a murderer? OMG; I am going to die! Now, if you just ran away from the house and never looked back, what do you think would happen the next time you came home? You would immediately begin to be afraid. The fear cycle and response would start again. "What if the person is still there? What if they brought their friends? OMG; I am going to die!"

Now, what if, that first time you came home, and you heard the loud noise, instead of running away, you decided to be brave and head upstairs, and investigate. (You know like the blonde in the horror films that you scream at when they are obviously walking into sure-fire danger... be the blonde.) So, you walk upstairs, and you suddenly realize that your son had come home early, and let in the cat. It was the cat that just knocked over the vase that was in front of the window. As soon as you realized that, you would immediately start to feel better, and think; **"Ahhhhh I didn't die."** The adrenaline that was previously coursing through your veins now starts to diminish, and your breathing starts to slow. Now, the next time you come home, instead of going back into the fear cycle, you breathe easy and think to yourself, "Remember when I thought there was a murderer in my house? Man was that ever crazy."

The point is, without the "Ahhhh, I didn't die" moment, you can not get over the fear. And this is true for your dog as well.

So now let's see this through the eyes of the dog.

You are walking your dog down the street, and you see that your neighbour has put out a brand new giant garden gnome. Very scary for a dog that has never seen a garden gnome. Your dog startles at the creepy elf.

Most people will have one of the two reactions to a dog's fearful response. Both extremes can have a very negative effect on the fearful dog.

Reaction #1

   You turn to the dog and immediately see that he is scared. You get down low at dogs level and try to coax your dog, cooing and saying, "it's okay buddy, you're okay." You pick up the dog and move around the gnome, or give the dog lots of space from the plastic troll and quickly make your way past it. On your way home, you make sure to cross the street, so your dog doesn't have to see that scary elf again!

Reaction #2

You turn to the dog and realize he is freaking out over that stupid ugly gnome and you shake your head and immediately pull the dog over to the gnome saying "Its just a gnome, don't be silly. I know it is a new lawn ornament, but you are being ridiculous."

As I mentioned, both scenarios can have an ill effect on the dog. The first is the "murderer in the house" scenario. By not allowing the dog to process the fearful stimulus and realize for himself that he did not die, you will have a dog that will go through the fear cycle again and again and again. So, moral of this story... let your dog be the blonde. 😉

In the second scenario, the dog is forced to "face" his fear, it is not being done on his terms. Forcing the dog to "go see" something when he is not ready to do so can, in a lot of cases, cause more trauma than the initial fear response.

I have a fear of spiders. If you put a spider on my hand and tell me to "get over it, it's just a little spider" I not only still will not like spiders; there is a good chance I am not going to like you either. (#spiderssuck)

So what does one do?

## The "Ahhh I Didn't die" Moment:

The natural response to a fearful stimulus is a cycle. It is a natural approach and retreat and approach and retreat until the dog can ascertain that there is in fact, nothing to be afraid of. Consider a litter of puppies all playing in the grass. Suddenly a plastic bag gets blown into their playpen. Immediately all the pups scatter (fear response: flight). Some may bark, some may go further than others, but eventually, you will see one or more of the pups start to make their way towards the bag. The bag moves again; they jump back, this time not quite as far. This repeats itself until finally, one brave pup grabs the bag in his mouth and starts shaking and playing with it. Before you know it, all the puppies are ripping around playing with the once terribly scary plastic bag. This cycle is how most dogs will deal with fear.

So let's go back to the scary garden gnome. The best way to let your dog cope with this fear is to allow for a natural approach and retreat. Now if your dog is on a leash, the leash itself may not be allowing the dog enough space to retreat. So your dog freaks out, jumps back to the end of the leash. The first attempt to approach the gnome may be a bit of a waiting game (depending on how comfortable your dog felt with the retreat distance). You have to wait this out. It is best NOT TO TALK TO YOUR DOG. I know this will be hard, because you want to say comforting things like "It's okay, You're okay. " However, when your dog is dealing with fear, he is in what I call the "right-brain" (we will cover this in more detail later), but essentially, the right brain is the instinctual brain of the dog. It is the flight/ fight/avoid/ "drives" (prey, sex, etc) part of the brain. The left side of the brain is the thinking side. The side that helps him understand obedience terms and English as a second language. When your dog is right-brained or instinctual, saying human words will not help them. I know we like to think it will, but they are just not able to access that part of their brain right now. So there is no point in talking to them. However, most people will keep talking. But I would be remiss if I didn't bring it up. Try to be silent, reliable, and confident for your dog. BE what you need the dog to be. Your dog will "hear" that. Allow the dog to approach and retreat. Now move slowly towards the object of the fear one step at a time, and by doing so, that will allow the dog to get closer but still retreat as necessary. However, the retreat will not be as far each cycle. Eventually, when the dog finally gets up to sniff and stays there, you know the cycle is complete, and you and your dog will be able to continue on your way.

*"Take the time it takes so eventually it takes less time"*

Pat Parelli Natural Horsemanship

How long does the fear cycle take? Every dog and every fear stimulus is different but generally the more fearful stimuli your dog encounters in his life, the quicker and easier the cycle. I will caution you to take Pat Parelli's advice and be sure to take the time. Do what needs to be done because left unchecked, fearful stimuli can become a trauma that you have to manage for the rest of your dog's life.

## Living with a Fearful Dog

A bullseye diagram (diagram 1 ) is the best way I can describe the same approach and retreat cycle as it relates to living with a fearful dog. Again, I should point out that there is absolutely nothing wrong with your dog. And that there are positives and negatives to owning an innately fearful dog, just as there are positives and negatives to owning an innately confident dog. For example, an innately fearful dog tends to be less likely to wander off, is more focused on their owner and as such can somewhat easier to obedience train with distractions. The innately confident dog, on the other hand, will be easily distracted and tends to wander away (because they are confident enough to do so). The confident dog will be more comfortable to take to different places like boarding kennels and be quite fine, whereas the fearful dog will more likely have separation anxieties about being away from their owners. See? — Positive and negatives to both. Both are equally awesome dogs.

Diagram 1

# BEYOND OBEDIENCE
WHERE YOUR DOG WANTS TO BE

## THE FEARFUL DOG

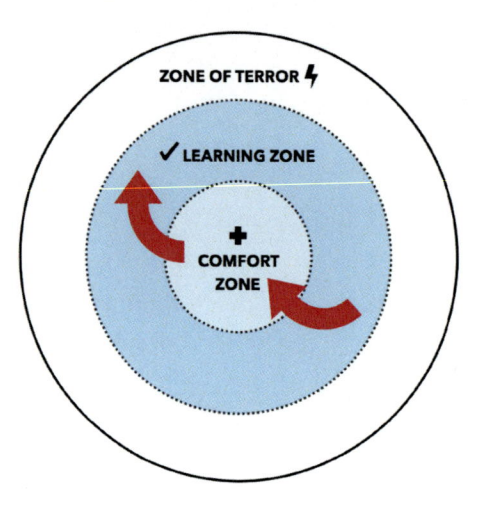

**ZONE OF TERROR**

✓ **LEARNING ZONE**

+ **COMFORT ZONE**

- **COMFORT ZONE** - only exists if there is a pattern of predictability
  - no learning takes place in the comfort zone (life learning)

- Dogs must be allowed to retreat back to the comfort zone to absorb what they have learned in the **LEARNING ZONE** ("that mailbox didn't kill me")

- Trauma happens in the **ZONE OF TERROR**

In the center of the bullseye is the COMFORT ZONE. The comfort zone may be as small as your dog's crate (incidentally, that is why I believe all fearful dogs should have a crate even if you don't close the door). Basically, the comfort zone is where your dog can predict the outcome of the environment with as close to 100% predictability as possible. Now, as your pup or your dog becomes more comfortable and has that pattern of predictability, that comfort zone may grow to the room or the house or the backyard. However, no learning takes place in the comfort zone. Now I am not talking about learning obedience. You should always start in the area your dog is most comfortable to teach them a new obedience command. I am talking about "life learning." You know stuff like, that mailbox isn't going to eat me, and that fire hydrant is a great place to pee. That sort of thing. So you must move your dog out of their comfort zone and allow them to experience things. And the more opportunity they get to do that, the larger the comfort zone becomes.

Now the next ring after the learning zone is the ZONE OF TERROR!!!! (said in an ominous voice). Terror is what happens when we push a dog too far. Flooding would be an example of potentially putting your dog in the zone of terror. And although there are times when flooding techniques have worked, if you do it wrong, you can end up creating a lifelong trauma.

Here is the critical thing to remember. We want to gently ease the dog out of the comfort zone into the learning zone to experience life and all the "OMG; I'm going to die! ... Ahhh, I didn't die moments. However, the dog must return to the comfort zone to "absorb" what they have learned. Always allow your dog some much-needed downtime in their favourite comfort zone after a busy day of life learning.

## Layered Stress
*Every dog has the potential to bite.*

As a professional working in the dog industry, I can't count how many times I have heard the phrase:

*" It happened out of nowhere!!"*

That is rarely the case. This "layered stress model" I learned from Chad Mackin of Pack to Basics in a seminar I attended a few years ago, compliments the fearful dog bullseye chart and allows people to see it from another angle.

When you are living with a fearful dog, you have to consider all the fearful stimuli your dog will encounter throughout the day. Each stimulus has the potential to bump your dog up the stress levels closer to the threshold in which your dog will bite. If your dog doesn't have adequate time or space to recover from the fearful stimulus, (ie comfort zone time) they remain at the new stress level, essentially layering each new stressor on top of the old ones. Then, as they linger just below bite threshold, one more seemingly insignificant incident will be the final push over threshold and "out of no where" your dog has his first bite.

LAYERED STRESS ( diagram 2)

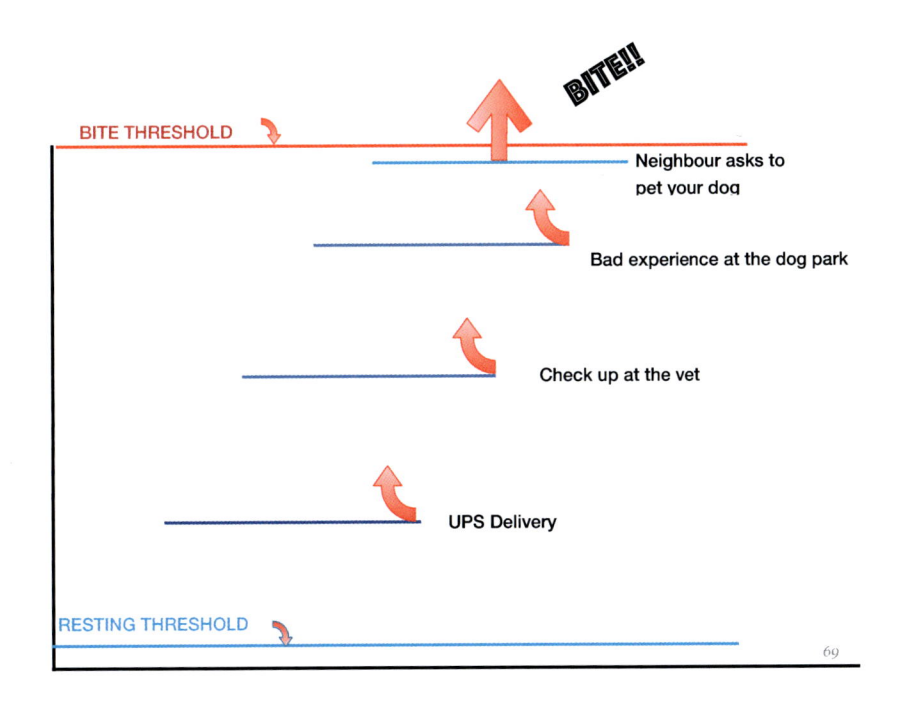

BITE!!

BITE THRESHOLD
— Neighbour asks to pet your dog
Bad experience at the dog park
Check up at the vet
UPS Delivery
RESTING THRESHOLD

Let's take the example in diagram 2. You dog wakes in the morning, and everything seems pretty chill until an unexpected delivery from the UPS guy. After a little barking episode your dog seems to settle down a bit. Shortly after you have to take your dog to the vet for a regular check-up. Your dog isn't bad at the vet clinic but hey; who's kidding who, the clinic can be a pretty stressful place. You decide to give your dog a run at the dog park to reward him for being so good, but there is an unfriendly dog there and you can tell your dog isn't having any fun. No one got hurt but you decided to leave early before anything happens. You get home and your neighbour is out mowing his lawn. He stops the mower comes over to say hi and bends down to give your dog a pet... and out of nowhere! SNAP! Your dog bites your neighbour! He's never done that before! What happened?
Layered stress happened.
But none of that matters because, now your dog knows how to bite, and you've lost trust in your dog. (And your dog has lost trust in you!)

**REMEMBER**~Don't over tax your fearful dog. Keep new experiences to a minimum and always make sure you allow your dog to go back to the comfort zone to absorb and relax.

# The Confident Dog
*And it's not about dominance*

All dogs are born innately something. Some are born confident: some are not. I find it interesting that when we come across a fearful or less than confident dog, we immediately assume something must have happened to them to make them that way. We don't have that same reaction when a dog is confident, or dominant as some may call it. When that happens, we have the opposite response and assume that the dog was " just born that way" and usually believe that there is nothing we can do about it. How interesting, huh? Why would we assume that confidence is genetic and yet being less than confident is not? I don't know the answer to that I only know this seems to be the common consensus amongst many of the dog owners I have met. I will say this though, whether you have a confident dog, or a fearful dog, all the above information about the Leadership Score Card, Relevance Score Card, Fulfillment Factor, all of it applies and works to build a better relationship with all dogs, regardless of their genetic tendencies towards confidence or not. The only difference is the motivation behind the work you do to build your Leadership Score Card or up your Relevance Score or Fulfilment Factor.

For example:

| MOTIVATION FOR: | CONFIDENT DOG | FEARFUL DOG |
|---|---|---|
| LEADERSHIP SCORE CARD | you are in charge | you've got their back |
| RELEVANCE SCORE CARD | You are worthy of being in charge | you understand them |
| FULFILMENT FACTOR | relieves frustrations | relieves anxiety |

When we are speaking of confident dogs, quite often people have a difficult time grasping the concept of needing to embrace proper leadership. It seems to be easier for the owners of the more fearful dog to step into the leadership role as the fearful dog has no desire to do it. But what about the dog that will happily accept the role of leader in the foreign land of Humansville? What happens to that dog, the human, and the relationship? Well, for humans, they tend to see unwanted bratty-like behaviour from their dog. That behaviour makes the owner quite frustrated. A previous client once told me, she hates the way the dog behaves! She sat in my office with tears in her eyes. "How is it possible to love my dog and hate him at the same time. He is literally ruining my life!" But here is the flip side of this coin. The dog also feels frustrated. Yes, it's true. Behind many of the unwanted behaviours lie a layer of frustration because the dog can not cope long term in the leadership role in Humansville. They just can't. They can't lead humans, mostly because we don't listen to them. And what happens when both parties of the relationship are frustrated? The relationship breaks down. Dogs get re-homed.

Many people will start to try to mend this relationship with obedience. Getting the dog to obey obedience commands is a surefire way to begin to change the balance of relationship with a confident dog. (It also gets you some of those Leadership Score Card points.) There is nothing wrong with that; in fact, I believe this is where obedience can help you out. I will say that this should all come AFTER you have done the foundational work mentioned in the previous chapters. Asking a dog to do a down stay when they are a confident dog is going to be met with resistance if your confident dog does not see you as 'worthy.' Your worthiness comes from all the foundational behaviour work you have done or will do in the first four chapters.

# The Right Brain/Left Brain Introvert/Extrovert discussion
*A different way to look at your dog*

I am going to credit Parelli Natural Horsemanship for this work. I was introduced to this concept of "HORSENALITIES" back when I was learning about horses, and I tried to relate it to dogs. Not an easy task when you are dealing with one glaringly big difference: horses are PREY and dogs are PREDATORS. Dogs also seem to have a lot of categories, like drives, and submission, dominance, etc. It seemed like it wasn't going to work, and I put it away for many years. But I recently came back to it, because of all the controversy over dog training terms. I thought it would be worth reinvestigating to try and simplify dog ownership and understanding your dog's behaviour. It will always be a work in progress, I think, but as someone who studies not only dog behaviour but also communication, I hope this will help some people find clarity.

## THE LEFT BRAIN
Simply put, the left brain is the "THINKING" side of the brain. This is the side that allows the dog to "understand" our English as a second language (obedience commands) and therefore helps the dogs cope with living in "Humansville"

## THE RIGHT BRAIN
The right brain would be the "INSTINCTUAL" side of the brain. This is the *fight, flight avoidance* and the "*drives*" of the dog ( prey, sexual, etc.)

> *It is important to note that dogs "flip" back and forth from right brain to left brain all the time. This concept is fluid.*

## INTROVERT
Not to be confused with the complex human definition of introvert/extrovert but for our purposes, I like to keep it simple by saying the Introverts don't want to move their feet.

## EXTROVERT
Move their feet. (Simple right 😉)

If you take a look at the chart (digram 3), I have noted some characteristics of the 4 categories. Starting in the upper left quadrant, we have the **Left Brain Introvert**. These dogs are quite clever but can be non-responsive. They may appear disinterested, and people will sometimes think these dogs are lazy and stubborn. I would categorize some of my Newfoundlands in the LB-I quadrant. The Newfoundland dogs are

quite often considered lazy because they tend to be slow-moving. However, they are extremely intelligent. That "stubbornness" is quite often passive resistance to training and can be quite challenging for many owners. Motivation is key to these guys, and you can often find it in your foundation of relationship. ( LEADERSHIP, RELEVANCE, and FULFILMENT)

In contrast to the LB- I is the **Left Brain Extrovert.** The LB-E is very smart and fast! They are playful and cheeky with a little mischievous added in. In my pack, I would categorize my Australian Shepherds here. These guys are great fun and extremely sharp. Try to keep up with them because if you don't, they will make up their own fun games with or without you! FULFILLMENT FACTOR is the key foundation block for these guys!

Diagram 3

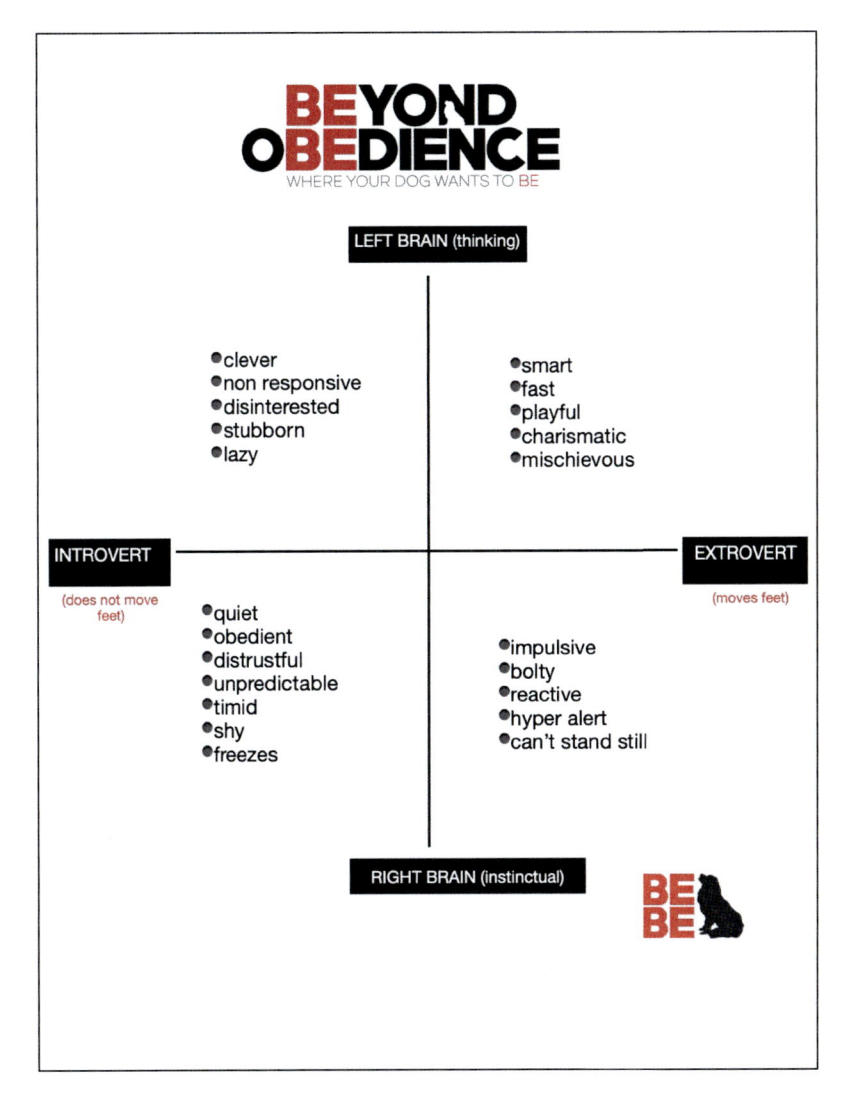

# BEYOND OBEDIENCE
WHERE YOUR DOG WANTS TO BE

**LEFT BRAIN (thinking)**

- clever
- non responsive
- disinterested
- stubborn
- lazy

- smart
- fast
- playful
- charismatic
- mischievous

**INTROVERT** (does not move feet)

**EXTROVERT** (moves feet)

- quiet
- obedient
- distrustful
- unpredictable
- timid
- shy
- freezes

- impulsive
- bolty
- reactive
- hyper alert
- can't stand still

**RIGHT BRAIN (instinctual)**

BE BE

Moving on to the bottom quadrants of the Right Brain dogs. Remembering that the right brain is the more instinctual side, the **Right Brain Introvert**, tends to be shy and quiet. These guys are timid and obedient with those they trust but very distrustful of all others. They tend to freeze when pushed too far but watch out for the explosion. Dogs like this need a firm advocate owner, one who will stand up for their dog no matter what. LEADERSHIP is what is needed here! Pot Cake dogs will fall into this category.

And finally, the **Right Brain Extrovert** is always on alert. These guys are flighty, impulsive, and skittish. If they run, they are hard to catch. RB-E's are described as "reactive" and need owners that can provide a predictable lifestyle (for the unconfident RB-E) with a lot of calming activities. For a confident RB-E, obedience is required to keep their prey drive in check! Understand that the right brain dog is all about survival. What does that mean to a dog? RELEVANCE / LEADERSHIP is your foundation blocks to this dog's zen.

## The Horses That Showed me the Way

What does natural horsemanship have to do with dogs?

My aha moment came when I first my Ferrier. He was so good with the horses, not just because it was his job, but he just seemed to "have a way" with them. I asked him where he learned this, and he introduced me to the world of Natural Horsemanship. By studying natural horsemanship, I began to see the importance of a relationship of co-operation instead of coercion. When you think about it, you need a cooperative relationship when you are dealing with a 1200 lb animal, don't you? I mean, if a horse doesn't want to go… they won't.

As I started working this concept with my horses, it helped me to see the different needs of my very different horses. At the time, I had a few horses. My gelding Magic would fall into the category of Left Brain Introvert. He was a "stubborn" horse and very "dull" to work with but oddly enough would also be the horse that would harass me in the field while I was helping my husband fix the fences. He would steal my hat and play with my hoodie. One day he walked off with the bucket of fencing supplies. I remember thinking, for such a dull horse, he certainly isn't dull in the field. It wasn't until I started understanding the concept of these Parelli Horsenalities that I realized that he wasn't dull, he was unmotivated by my training sessions, and I had to up my game.

In contrast, my Quarter Horse mare Flame is a Right Brain Extrovert. The slightest movement could make her jumpy.

She was challenging to get into a trailer (I think she saw it as the steel box of death). She didn't like any changes in stalls or paddocks or routine, and she was bolty and flighty when I rode her. With her, I learned I had to slow down, use small movements, and of course, build trust.

Later in my work with dogs, I soon realized that I was using the same or similar techniques. Fearful dogs that would freeze, I knew I had to get them to move their feet. Slow, stubborn dogs, I now saw the challenge of "how do I get you to think I am interesting?" The flighty, bolty, reactive dogs, I now knew not to bother with the obedience; they were not able to hear that just yet. I need to "snap" them out of right-brain and back to left-brain so that they could understand me. And honestly, it stopped me from trying to analyze it in dog terms. Is he being dominate? Is she submissive? What drive are they in?

Now behaviour isn't this simple. I realize that. However, I found this to be a great start to understanding dogs' reactions. Keep it simple so that you can respond to your dog's reactions in the moment and then dog behaviour 'geek out' and analyze it later in your spare time. ( At least that is what I do 😉)

# Conclusion
*The journey to a better relationship has just begun.*

I want to take this opportunity to mention that this is a book about *LIVING* Beyond Obedience. I want to emphasize the living part. This book isn't a dog training book or even a how-to book. It's an idea book — a new way of looking at life with a dog. Learning how to understand your dog and transplant yourself in the dog's mind, and by doing so, you will naturally move towards a more connected, empathetic relationship with your dog. When you start to practice the concepts outlined in this book and live within the F.O.R. Framework, I think you will begin to see a massive shift in what it means to share a relationship of mutual respect, trust, and understanding. But it is a life long journey. Enjoy the ride.

To your Relationship,

~T

MORE LBO OPPORTUNITIES:

- Relationship Remedy: Online Coaching Program for Dog Lovers
- Living Beyond Obedience: The Essentials Course: Online Course for getting started living beyond obedience.
- LBO Monthly Membership: Monthly Membership with discussions and interviews, book club and more all about Living Beyond Obedience.

Visit our website: www.beyondobedience.ca for more information!

Manufactured by Amazon.ca
Bolton, ON